THE S
(Sailing

M000081865

"Mommy, I know how you suffer so and I hate watching what this innocent accident and its daily consequences has done to you. I know that you know that my life is not my physical body, though it was once encased within that beautiful body, through which, in our mutual human days, we facilitated our contact in the physical world. However, the true contact comes from our souls each within a physical body, until it is not through physical death, through that transition and into a radiant higher body of light. In essence, the soul becoming, stretching, expanding even bigger into that true body. True life. Completeness. Life elevated. Continuously brightening. At that point, that contact is still soul to soul, one within a physical body and one in a body of light. That is a significant truth that you hold. I am alive. Present. Current. With you. I will never leave your side. As on your left side, it is my right. While you cross through turbulent, hurricane infested seas of grief in my physical absence, and while you commune with me and spend time with me in my spiritual life, know that I am so in love with you, Momma, and so, so proud of you. Keep walking Mommy. I call you forward..."

~ Kayleigh Mooney

Preamble: First She Had To Build A Skiff

In an instant, a life obliterated, with the apex of grief rifling through a parent's spirit. In her physical life, throughout her physical life, and on that day, just fifteen years, three months and two days old; brilliant, a deep thinker, lover of all light, innocent, hilarious, dynamic, compassionate, courageous, faithful, smart, talented and joyous. Trying to cross a street to come home, innocently struck by a car in an accident she did not create; having made a good decision at that time to come home, and having felt perfectly safe with every right to feel safe; with the driver of the car feeling safe driving; obscured from the other, blocked by telephone poles, an immediate and instant collision, striking the pavement where she lay, in her father's arms, passing from life to life while her mother ran to her side.

Stolen. Robbed. Unfair. Arms had held her just hours before. Her arms now empty of her daughter's physical presence. At what length to endure. At what length would she turn to learn the adjustment. Hemorrhaging emotion. Bleeding soul light. Cursing breath.

An ocean lay before her. Her daughter somewhere beyond the waves of grief. First, she needed to build a boat. From her ribs she fashioned the hull. From her womb the sheeting to waterproof the floor. From her bones the planks that, once nailed into the frame, would present a powerful spearhead of resolve to cut and jag through the world's most powerful and untidy waves. From her eyes and her lips and her heartache and her soul, she weaved wooden oars, fitting only her hands. Greasing the components and the joints of the boat with her mother's blood and milk. She painted the skiff, from end to end, inside and outside, with her indigo and pearl smeared tears.

Focused on the golden horizon line, she pushed the heavy boat across the sand, scratching its newly minted boards, a natural consequence of the toiling before her. She lurched the boat into the shallows of all she had known, ripping her hands on the splinters, managing poorly in those first moments to control the boat's first crawl in the water as she struggled to throw herself into its cradle; its unprotected hull. The wooden boat grazed up and down on the sand in the shifting water, banging against the ground, lifting into the waves, until she turned the nose outward toward oblivion and into the dangerous unknown. She ventured off into a dark midnight sea, rowing through fear and doubt and horror, with a hurricane tempest uncaged roiling about the atmosphere, and to this point, uncontested.

Off within that golden horizon, blazing in the purest joy, Kayleigh called out to her, a smile peacefully encouraging her, from that distance, "Mommy! Mommy! I am here!"

SPIRITO OCEANIC BLEED

"Spirito Oceanic Bleed"

Adrift, listless flailing,
Abhorring crooked dream on which I'm failing,
No, Lord, the veins are draining,
Into the sea where my soul is staining,
The waves...

...Cannot restrain nor restrict this bleeding,
The grief steam engine demands constant feeding,
Here on this beach and humanly restricted,
I stared off to the horizon,
To the glorious...

...To the mystic...

...The spirit of the sea speaks to the soul,
And it is speaking clearly to mine,
And so I search for my way across,
Strapping onto my back this personalized cross...

...I can hear her pining in the cloud line chime,

..."Mommy, meet me where the sea touches the sky."

"Mother Light"

In whose womb she grows,
Protected by rib bones,
A light for the ages,
Resonates in the chamber,
Where a baby - she glows,
An angel with tiny toes,
Clings to her Mother's soul;

Where they intertwine,
Every cell, every line,
Becomes both of them,
For all of time,
For this baby - she glows,
As gravity pulls,
A changing of worlds comes,
Yet she has always known,
How to cling to Mother's soul.

"How Did I Get Here"

I stumbled out from a flash of trauma,
Deposited on a desolate, tangled physical beach,
On the whereabouts of the unknown,
From where I was - now so very far,
As far away as me waving up at stars,
To try to close the gap in the air,
And not truly comprehending -

How did I get here;

Deposited on another planet,
Dropped upon its stony surface,
With no map and no reconnaissance,
And with no valid purpose,
I scream and my voice cowls the wind,
How, oh Lord -

How did I get here;

And once upon this jagged land,
Where promise and hope are slain,
There is nothing but a hard road,
For the remainder of my days,
Reminiscing of the happy times,
And the love and lives we shared,
Wishing I could unwind time,
To wish me out of today,
And the torture present here.

"In the Forest of the Lost"

The acrid steam of the swamp wafts,
Lushly bloomed on a humid rash,
As stagnant, as silent as the Spanish Moss,
Hangs from the branches like bundles of sage green gauze,
A possum hides in the webbing,
As the Cardinal flies across,
And lands in floral branches,
And sings of rebirth in the forest of the lost;

She thanks morning visions in the change,
And washes dawn's canvas in a salty rain,
Spreads colorful contrasting liquid acrylic paints,
Across the day and its radiant face,
Knowing such freedom in the highest, brilliant life;

Sometimes the centuries hide in seconds,
Like a termite colony unbeknownst in bark,
Sometimes the hallway fills with smoke,
And the optimism goes dark,
And the trauma beckons,
And the wounded heart,
Folds underneath its own weight;

In the forest of the lost,
There is forward only one way,
The thickets of the passed press to her backbone,
Standing on this beach,
While the shoreline decays,
Under her feet,
Of all she had known,
And believed in before,
Before the worst type of tragedy,
Cast her grieving on this desolate shore.

"In the Aftermath of Night"

And if the morrow rise sullen,
Or bruises blue the fields of skin,
No terrain - not renown,
Slowly flowers sprout from well-traveled chagrin,
Where the seedlings dance of water,
And the ocean floors shimmer golden white,
We find hope like oily polished stones,
Call our feet to bathe,
In the aftermath of night.

"A Moment Alone"

Just leasing an adjacent space to get away from people,
These Human mosquito swarms,
That clog the airways with their self-effusive complaints,
And Winged in self-indulgent uniforms,
I walk through a flock of a thousand cartwheeling gnats,
And hear their humming voices as I step off into the void.

"Night Sitting Seaside and Grief"

Silence fed a deadening sea,
A shade darker than me,
In the long, quiet night,
Under clover-lime moonlight…

…Intertwined with my flesh like filigree;

Tiny beads and twisted threads,
My thoughts and pains and tears,
Bundled in rusty barbed wire webs,
These knots - they refine me,
They find me grieving,
For you,
And shed of dream, I find no sleep,
And in its callous thieving,
I stare at the deafening sounds on the sea...

...A near motionless ocean ripples towards me,
The windless surface crawls to the beach,
And trickling water echoes on the sand,
Louder than I can breathe...

...My life, My Love,
I listen for my heartbeat,
It, like a shadow, hides among the henges of my teeth,
Screams from the flesh of my womb…

…While a purple water blackens.

"Whispers of the Spanish Moss"

The ghosts of an ocean's moor,
Their phantom fingers lurk in the quandary of the fog,
Leaving dewdrops like seedlings,
On tree skeleton logs,
In the tangles of the branches,
Of oaks and cypress in the marshes and bogs,
That throng behind the high white dunes,
Living threaded curtains frame the beachfront,
In the sea breeze,
They listlessly sway...

...The Spaniard's Moss like bundles of silky straw,
Crawl across the clouds in filigree sprawl,
Gather in the cracks of the tabby walls,
And hang from the ancient oaks,
And whisper down the forest halls...

...To those who are awake.

"The Intruder"

The intruder lurks unchecked under mask,
And broken screen,
The intruder, framed in open sash,
Prowls the soul along the seams,
The intruder is as familiar as a family member,
Is to me -

It beds down in the conscience and brews its morning tea,
And probes across emotion for signs of fragility,
It scans the mind for weakness, for any entrance it can see,
Whether nightmare or by daytime,
Or through the doorway of a dream -

In the darkness it is stealthy,
This intruder and its greed,
In the darkness it is healthy,
For the fear on which it feeds,
In the darkness I awaken,
To confront elusive thief,
And face him in my hallway,
Armed with faith to fight this grief...

"Looking Out Across a Temped Sea"

I close these eyes and listen for her life,
Like a rhythmic sound torches the ocean,
It sparks the waves in the heat of daylight,
And echoes through the fluid acres of the open seas…

…As the wind disturbs the calm surface,
And the choppy waves arrive.

"And Hope, A Victim of the Drought?"

Compel me, the shroud of constant doubt,
Where were all the rowboats hidden,
In the caustic years of drought,
As if all the roots have rusted, reddish into ash,
And no viability registers on this barren patch,
It is just the story within this song,
That you try to sing along,
When all hope - all hope has been dispatched;

It climbs its way through crevasses and clay,
Worms its fingers through the soil and finds the light of day,
It works its way through shale and stone,
Breathing marrow into bones,
Well aged...

...It builds upon its hidden strength and bursts upon the stage,
Sprouting green leaved seedlings in the aftermath of rain,
Never losing itself amidst the stench of dead terrain,
Rising, it has risen, for it has never gone away.

"Without You (Physically)"

I long for you as if you are my breath,
That without you, with no air through my chest,
I would die one thousand times,
Die one thousand deaths,
In each second without you,
Without my breath;

Though rib, deep marrow, my flesh, this chest,
I carried you as soul and cell and human mesh,
All converged within my womb,
Holy, like a morning psalm,
Now your physical absence,
Is too much to bare each second long…

…But I breathe in your light,
Your mother needs you,
In this and every life,
So we find the way of wisdom,
And we find the space in this chest (too tight),
And we find each other,
In the halo of a radiant night.

"A Century, A Second"

It takes a century to track the life of a ravaged second,
In those moments,
A century of living, with all of its lessons,
As if time was frozen,
As the soul itself exerts,
Itself,
And the in-breath, for out, reverts,
Into the next second,
Tied together one by one,
Into hours,
Chained like metal tears into the necklace of a raging day,
And another into others into a month,
That scavenged its way,
Across the broken ground,
And evolved across these earths into one year,
And another,
Vacant of scent and sound.

"Deep Soul Sore"

This road is not meant for humans,
No human should be forced to endure,
No human experience was meant to include,
What lay beyond this shore,
Yet here I am on this pathway thinning,
Crawling a few inches more,
Yet here I am where no human should be,
Standing in the cemetery of oyster shells,
Panic clothed,
With brackish mud clogging my pores,
Mortal in my cellular structure,
Mortal come what may come,
Mortally wounded...

...And foot and...

...Deep soul sore.

"The Morning Life"

A rash of rage it ranges forth,
Taking on the psyche of a dangerous course,
Taking on the Light of this World,
With weapons of questions and recriminations,
For how can such a lovely family end up in this situation -

I am speechless, Oh Lord,
With a silence that I can't afford,
If the world could try to hurt me more...

...It would come up short –

For there is nothing worse,
Than this sadness for my child for whom I mourn,
Take me to the diamond shores,
Where there stands a gold encrusted door,
And lay my body before it - on its floor,
And let this pain melt away into the morning life.

"I Am Coming, Kayleigh"

Your mother is here,
Your mother is coming,
Your mother I fear,
Won't know how to cross,
Your mother is hurting,
Such heartache erase,
The youth from your mother,
Now lines on my face,
Tell of the tail of physical loss,
No parent should embrace,
Yet innocent the night it came,
Where my life was destroyed,
And replaced with such pain,
But worry not, my daughter,
Your mother is coming,
Your mother is here,
Though bound in the deepest despair,
Your mother is coming...

...Your mother is here.

"A Moon Warrior"

I stand knee deep in the shallows,
Like a moon warrior holding back the tide,
The grief, it crashes into me,
I absorb the mighty blows,
Water that cuts with gashing force of mercurial blade,
On occasion I collapse,
And reset my frame and feet,
Rescued in respite,
My stand slightly more firmly each time I fall,
Strengthening in the punishment,
Moored, though in shuffling sands,
And man my post with a shield of reconciliation,
And a sword of light that sparks,
As it slices through the darkness,
Opening up the grief...

...Like a zipper opens to the fullness...

...Of life...

...And each time the darkness returns,
To swallow me…

…I invest the full power of this holy knife.

"The Pain That Lies Beneath"

If the midnight was blood and the darkness my veins,
There are moments so grievous,
No amount of morning can relieve this pain,
But for the grace of the bounty moon,
No matter crescent silver or full,
As I swallow the waves,
Vomiting salt,
I dream the consequence of its pull...

...Drifting into another new day,
The first thought always upon me,
Before my first full breath awake...

...My daughter has been physically killed,
The scabbard of my soul, it screams,
As the light of my spirit shakes,
In the condemned dereliction strewn from a mother's grief,
Before the body rises,
While my feet are still asleep,
I am quite aware...

...Of the pain that lies beneath.

"Behind These Dreamless Eyes"

I may smile in a greeting,
I may laugh, seemingly engaged,
I may wax and be entertaining,
But you do not see this cage,
It holds a panicked hyena,
That circles a metal box with rage,
For my daughter has been physically killed,
At fifteen years of age!

The world with its current events,
And its headlines and its gate,
Only those who similarly suffer,
Can understand this life sentence,
And this cruel fate;

And they ask me, "how are you?"
And their eyes invade this sorrow,
While their eyes avoid the time,
That support could only borrow,
And they ask me, "are you better?"
And I smile,
While the harm lay sealed and contained,
Aphron stereo wilt and clang,
Buzzing in the belfry of this dreamless pain,
Senselessly the reason abandoned,
In the words that so easily stray,
You have asked me an impossible question…

…What is it that you would like me to say?

"Please"

Please, if you can summon your voice,
Louder than my mind's noise,
It would help me in my current state,
As I punch and push and pirouette through barricades,
That grief has fringed with barbed wire and wicked blades;

Please, if you can drum up an echo to chase down the wind,
And ring your song in the wind chimes to wash out chagrin,
It would relieve at least some of this thieving weight;

And all the sounds of emptiness,
They bed themselves into the firmament,
Across the fields where the flocks of grief release,
I scream your name, compelled, and to my knees...

...I row onward while the blisters claim their ranks,
Peeling off the flesh of my fingers, thumbs,
And suck at the reservoir of my strength...

...Then, an intuitive truth returns,
Shaped in the grace of your delicate voice,
And the faith, it, though weakened,
Strums like pulsing beacon,
And my back returns to its post...

..."Mommy...

...You are amazing, keep coming, I am right here..."

"Tempest in a Teapot"

Buckled down with eyes fully wide,
Slamming down the next slope of another gigantic wave,
And blasting into the heaving waters,
As the hull and trough collide;

And as the ocean swirls into a circular divide,
With no safe place nor curl nor crest in which to hide,
I open the arms and sternly submit,
As the tempest in a teapot,
Is the ocean to this skiff…

…Your Mother is coming,
Your Mother is here…

…In the lifting,
Like a million full moons in a galactic chandelier,
In the polar shifting,
On a solar wind,
Within the grace of this moment,
Ranging towards each other,
With intention declared,
We wrap our soul's arms entwined,
In this sacred space that we long to share…

…Drifting in the shallows on a glassy,
Gentle,
Whispering,
Trickling tide.

"In the Mouth of Wind"

As the mouth of wind, blossom wide,
Warmer than the air it glides,
In which the message here unfolds,
In whispers coded to the soul...

...In the higher ear where land is sky,
Where the ocean tongue clears the cloudy eye,
I know that you are sitting here,
In this quiet space that we both share...

...Though the ship of life, the vessels changed,
We were never parted, not estranged,
And you, though now in higher light,
We continue the journey of our lives...

...Hand in hand and feet to feet,
From a baby's cradle to the deadly street,
Though we did not end on that fateful night,
We intensely changed but continued in spite...

...Of the ending of your physical life...

...Of the beginning of your spirit life...

...In the mouth of wind,
Hold me, Darling...

...Alight.

"Resonance of Light"

In a blinding flash, the tone of which is so bright,
It crashes through the barrier of sound,
And vibrates in resonance,
And vacillates between the miraculous and the profound,
Leaving a fingerprint of her lovely voice,
Unrestricted, unbound,
For when light resonates across the dimensions,
It makes this deep, humming sound,
That vibrates skin with spirit tones,
And bridges communication,
Between two loving souls.

"Dear Daughter"

She holds me when I cry,
Picks me off the floor when I,
Collapse, collapse to my knees -

She guides my wary eyes,
Empowers my steps when I,
No longer sense my feet under me -

I hear her dance in the wind chimes,
Sense her warmth with me when I,
Stretch the pen into poetry stream -

She holds her mother when I cry,
Unfolds the path before my eyes,
Dear Daughter, lead my soul,
Onward,
Row with me, my Daughter,
This skiff to bridge the gap of space and time,
This skiff of my flesh and blood,
With hands so tired they grow blind,
With heart so heavy it, instead of beating, grinds...

...Down into sleep while the boat tips and lags,
On thirty foot midnight waves,
That only tack,
At your command.

"Saturn's Lullaby"

As is the case in a life sentence as this,
Each day erupts with seething grieving,
And hidden gifts,
The dissonance of disbelieving,
A soul bursting at the seams,
And seething;

She reads the eyes and signals poignant song,
That strums the air as she opens her palm,
And reaches to me in morning lift,
A subtle atmospheric shift,
Yet here all along;

Bewitched with expectations,
And here in the salty cauldron,
Why dream a dream that dreaming braced,
With emptiness,
Stray, charmed and mystic,
Mesmerize even the vagaries of life,
And the heartache - its strangling fingers,
Wrap around the trunk of the neck,
Besiege me with barbs and bristle,
Only to open that door to freedom,
Taste its lightning waves…

…That strike you like nothing else in this human dimension;

Under the bloom of Saturnian System,
Rhea and Mimas and Tethys and Titan traverse,
Pursued in the intricacies of gravitational flight,
And once upon a time another was dispersed,
To spread out like golden light,
To puncture the gloomy veil of the night;

She is a miracle worker,
She is channeling glory,
She is God's own light,
She strains to break through,
The chains of a human mind,
She strains to communicate,
Like a pulsating star blinks across the fields of night;

Crisscross our dimensions,
Crisscross with intention,
Moving around the edges to reach out to the other's hand,
We find that touch,
Though you are in your spiritual body,
And I...

...I am tucked still in humankind.

"A Bridge to the Everything"

Awash in the labyrinth of grief uninvited,
Like a river of cement that clots,
Tying the soul up into knots,
I choke on the hours of the day…

…And you, you hold the key to break apart the stone,
You will never let me face the darkness alone,
A bridge to the everything,
You are, the intercession, my daughter,
And the guardian of my soul,
You lift my eyes from the road,
A blinding light to which I am exposed,
Sings in your lovely voice...

…And I here you say,

"I am wrapping my wind around you,
I am wrapping my love around you,
Protecting you, Mommy, you,
Wrapping you with my life,
Wrapping you with my arms,
Wrapping you with my light,
Wrapping you with my heart,
Mommy, you, Mommy, you..."

…Between these two worlds I sail toward you,
With the songs of our lives that we sing,
On your bridge of light,
That leads me to the everything.

"Silver Confetti"

Shockingly bright,
She is no passive light,
That hangs over the night,
Just pleased with her glow,
Not this one, no -

She is active in flight,
And engaged in this life,
And heals the ways of this soul,
For she lovingly knows...

...The fields of glittering silver that glow upon my sea,
These rivers of stars that flow within me,
Entangled in my galaxies,
That loom in luminescence in her palm -

She is courageous and powerful,
Centuries strong,
She has learned to bridge two worlds and its wound,
She is the glowing reflection of God's own light,
That pools with love's perfection,
And radiates in her mother's eyes,
And mother's womb,
That illuminates the open sea,
Like dancing silver confetti,
Beamed from blooming glances of an ocean's hunting moon.

"Limited and Limitless"

Through a self-centered lens,
Their eyes they defend,
What they cannot see,
They cannot know,
Through the self-centered lens,
Their judgments toll,
But they cannot breathe,
The air that we breathe,
Tucked in the furthest corners of the soul;

Yet what I cannot with these eyes see,
Is not the limit of what I know,
For I see with my spirit,
I see with my soul,
I see you in your gowns of love,
Lighting up the world,
I see you, my beautiful daughter,
My beautiful girl;

We are not as limited as one may seem to be,
There will be no limit placed on me;

If never there was a woman,
Nor such a wound that licked at the light,
If never the heaven's curse could beguile the weathered face,
If never the life could absorb what the human was not meant to
embrace,
If never the burden so heavy,
If never I make it across…

…Kayleigh,
I will make it across,
I will make it across,
I will make it across.

"Streams of Living Water"

And she, with liquid diamonds in the tropic oceans of her voice,
Sing in silver blue and green and gold and gemmed turquoise,
A prism of sunrise bursting,
Our hearts - quenched and thirsting,
For the chorus of a crystal sea,
For hope to see our way through grief,
The streams of living water,
That her sweet voice brings to me…

…It gives me the strength…

…Strength enough to breathe.

"No Severance"

No severance has slain this air,
No space exists that we don't share,
Though I yearn with outstretched, empty hand,
When I forget that you are here;

No easy task while still encased,
And skinned within this human face,
To be both in Heaven's domain,
While tied to this earthly, lowly place;

Yet no severance has actually occurred,
No separation from my little girl,
Thought tragedy took your physical life,
The physical torture is not your light;

Hold my hand and walk this day,
An angel with God's loving grace,
Present with your mother here,
For no severance has slain this air.

"Astral Traveler"

This mesh, its fabric, its cloth,
Stretched across,
Blood and bone,
The flesh, encase this glow,
And speak, oh brilliant soul,
Wrapped within this skin,
And centuries old,
This galaxy of gold,
It breathes -

This home is as fleeting as turbulent wind,
We travel without and we travel within,
We travel the road of the sky,
Lit by the stars in our eyes,
And the lanterns of our meditative sleep...

...Sleep it comes heavily to me,
An astral traveler,
On a journey across an uncharted sea...

"Nothing Will Stop This Mother..."

Leaning into the natural forces of total destruction,
Walking fiercely, directly through the chaotic maelstrom of a
hurricane,
The texture of this beast - it ranges through my blood,
It flattens my bones in the torrent,
As I strain every life that has come before,
To be with you -

Not knowing the direction, visually,
Through the cyclical blades of wind,
Instead, I close these human eyes and follow the eternal vision
of the soul,
Through the howling, deafening roar,
And I see you there off in the sunlight, on our pleasant beach,
on the other side,
With turquoise waters and purple sky,
Radiating with joy and love and encouragement and pride,
And you see me here in the spinning sheets of this storm,
Fighting toward you,
With the love of a mother blazing in my eyes,
That no hurricane resists,
No hurricane defies.

TRAVELING IN
A BOAT OF LIGHT

"The Circle That Matters"

I show myself to the circle that matters,
I show myself to those then awake,
I show myself to those of compassion,
To those with a sacred trait;

For those that I have chosen,
For my family in such tender need,
I show myself to this circle of faithful,
To carry these messages that I speak.

"Grieving Mother Seethe"

A mountain of cloud crumble,
A mouth of smoke through the sunlight melt,
A perfectionist stumbles,
Just as she throws her charms at a wishing well,
And watch the coin she fumbled,
Bounce upon an earthen floor,
Unsung;

Fill my lungs with cement,
And have me swim against the tide,
I face a hurricane and a tornado interlocked in pirouette,
Raging toward me in an open liquid field,
And you ask me to hide,
The pendulum flows from grief to rage,
Sleek knife sleeps like armor under my tongue,
Armed with lethal blade;

No bridge we need to build,
For the structure already exists,
In the love in our hearts,
And resolve in clenched fists,
For nothing shall keep us apart;

I will rip away the thunder,
And burn away the tidal wave,
I will tackle the mighty equator,
And wrap the poles around its face,
I will stop at nothing,
To feel your embrace,
For I am a grieving mother,
A woman wrapped in tender cloaks of sorrow seething,
And struggling forward toward…

…The pulsing promise of your grace.

"Of Another Sky"

And here the air, a scented dream, fills the soul as I pass,
And here I walk upon an ever brittle sheet of flexing glass,
That separates this earth from a higher earth,
One soiled and spiked with light,
And not of sediment and metals and dirt,
Barefoot, I step across the great divide,
With damaged feet and a heavy heart that hurts,
It hurts,
It really hurts...

...My wounded eyes, in aching glance, arch,
Into the burden where space and time collide,
Longing to unclothe my quilted, bloodied, matted wings,
And place them, sacredly,
With purple lilacs and lavender and lilies,
And a prayer,
At the altar on the gold crusted threshold of another sky.

"I Suffer..."

With a million barbs - choke the feet of each new day,
Metal vines that tie so tight - breath so shallow it suffocates,
The fear is incomprehensible,
My aching soul indefensible,
I pray...

And I raise my eyes in the cold veil of morning,
And I pull the day on like I put on cold, iron clothing,
And march into the maelstrom,
Of sorrow, of sadness, of a mythical dismay...

Panic presses the release gently of grief seeds,
These are soft tears flowing freely now,
Without a sob - without a sound,
Without a prompt – breathe hallowed ground,
Planted in the ocean like hungry space black holes,
That dwell between these precious eyes;

In the distance, my daughter's brilliant gaze,
My only hope,
I throw myself, a coin, into the wishing well of the ocean,
In a tiny boat,
With little chance of surviving the crossing,
How tormenting the truth of suffering,
Each day...

...Daily I face.

"Flaming Comets Of Cloud"

Blurred, the ears sense a troubled air,
Swirling in a tepid atmosphere,
The blades of light look like tongues of fire,
Fueled by a wind that takes them higher,
As they rise,
Like flaming comets of cloud alight the skies,
Like burning dreams that dry the eyes,
And as I fall,
They rise...

...The weather escalates into detriment,
Over craters, lunar typhoon swept,
And wiped away a desert, stripped and scraped,
Grinding down an entire landscape,
In the eyes,
And the tower built with grief I cry,
Brick by tear brick and rising high,
So tall the structure punctures the sky,
Like flaming comets of cloud explode...

...Sending me scurrying into the shelter-less bones...

…Of the stern…

…Of this skiff.

"Today's Tsunami Of Belly Grief"

It is just like watching the waves from within the waves,
Each day,
They come slashing,
Crashing into and over and underneath,
Linking the seconds into a panic chain,
That weave into the matrix of a day,
Where the balancing act congeal,
Tips forth and back,
Across this field unleashes the battle to survive,
It rage,
It rage,
It rage;

What am I to do, my child...

...Placed in the exact position from which there is no escape,
The essence of true powerlessness,
In what could be my watery grave,
I cannot give up, no I cannot,
I raise our sails and harness the wind,
Riding just one more wave,
That uncurls from within chagrin.

"The Haunting Bedevilments"

The conscience guards the subterranean gardens,
In the waxy clay fields of the hardened mind,
Slashed and sutured by the stitches of time,
He with vulgar replacement for breath,
Snorts to filter oxygen,
From the wretched air that offered him sustenance,
No safety he here hopes to find;

And grief incarnate from phantom form,
Abuses your personal space,
Through its taunting and its scorn,
And its penetrating blade,
Impaling its fiery finger in the small of your backbone,
Melting your gravely weakened spine,
It gives way,
Collapse the cage that protects the heart,
Under the sheer weight of heartache.

"Repair Me"

It is, though immutable, in constant flux,
The same ebb and flow as in other natural law,
I have been stretched beyond my skin,
Strapped by deadening exhaustion,
I have been kept greatly upset,
By life's consequences and causes,
And the infrequent windows for pauses,
And the limited chances to retreat,
Leaving me staggered,
Nearly nauseas,
But each time the punch lands,
I breathe and expand,
And although sometimes instinctively cautious,
I open my trembling hands,
And allow the Father's light to repair me.

"Ultraviolet Tidal Stray (The Flesh Of This Ocean)"

My human eyes, they deceive me,
When I close these human eyes I breathe me,
See the sea in ultraviolet,
Brisk smoke, it steams transparently,
Apparently,
In private golden strands,
That thread with lilac fire water,
That God holds within His hands;

For in the corners of one's higher vision,
In the sacred index of refraction lives,
A color that streams from the sun,
Beyond the rainbow's visible bands;

Breaking light into spectral components,
The colors the eyes can breathe,
There is much more beyond what these human eyes perceive,
It is its own unique wavelength,
It is further than purple is purple,
Its color burns the horizon in a hidden wave,
And lifts the senses,
Into an indescribable dimension,
It is love itself,
The flesh of this ocean,
That dwells and swells in dips,
With the tidal stray.

"My Sanctuary"

Will you visit Saturn and take photographs for me,
And then in meditation pass those images to me,
Will you swim the nebula, the ancient solar seas,
Will you mark vacation spots for when I am finally freed,
Will you walk on Titan and leapfrog galaxies,
And whisper tails of miracles within my open dreams...

...While on this imperfect skiff,
Taking on water,
I sleep and as I sleep...

...Will you gather favorite spots into itinerary,
Wherever you want to take me,
When too transition comes,
Will be my sanctuary.

"Saturn's Children"

A million strings of light entwined,
Intertwined,
Release of intergalactic interferons,
To prevent the decay of mystery,
Saphron thistles boiled down into sentry moon,
Titan, epic and grand in stature,
Hidden beneath the veil of angel's wings,
Shields the gardens of paradise,
And extols enchantment's find;

Underneath the golden cloud fields and a pastel steam,
There are fields and hills cut by a maze of lovely streams,
And oceans bequeathed to the sediment of dreams,
Flowers cling to tree trunks and hang from the lush canopies,
And fill the air with fragrance of lilac seas;

Your father has told me of the space whales migrating,
Through the Saturnian System,
I have wanted so desperately to see them,
But meditation can be so frustrating,
He sees them with you on the beachfront,
When the dusk lights on Exuma Infinite are fading,
They call to each other he claims,
In a family melody much like ours,
And touch each other across millennia,
And a million oceans of a billion stars,
And graze in the nebula mangroves,
Where Tethys and Mimas are,
They lay at your feet while you bless them,
And continue their sea bound chart.

"This Moment's Fold"

I earn my place upon your proud wall,
I earn my place within our daily beads,
I earn my place in constant contact,
Fulfilling my daughter's needs -

I earn my place when trudging forward,
Dreaming of release,
I earn my place moving towards,
Your higher, brilliant peace -

I earn my place beside my daughter,
I earn my place within her soul,
For everything we are together,
Lives within this moment's fold.

"Breathe You"

I breathe your light,
In deep meditation,
Like breathing in a galaxy's nursery,
A million tiny stars flow in the oxygen,
That sparkle in the channels of my blood,
Glittering like acres of diamonds cascading in the sun...

...Invigorating the wounded soul,
Heavy in its shoes on this earthly domain,
Then a heaving step transforms in flight,
Lifting the spirit like the morning shifts the night,
Back and forth,
Each breath exhaled,
All day long,
Each breath a life,
Each breath from death inhaled.

"She Is..."

An ocean swirling with radiant light,
It's heaving waves crash with beach and ignite,
Illuminating every grain of sand like the sun,
Like a billion fireflies captured in a lightning's tongue,
She is...

...In the air about me she sings of this light,
That lifts me in her rivers of love to a higher vibration,
For this human condition - an important station,
Is but a temporary home -

She looks beyond the veil of my human flesh,
And fills my frontiers with a daughter's precious gold,
For she is teaching me - soul to soul,
The ways of this road,
She is...

...An ocean swirling with God's own light,
A constant beckon for her Father's life,
She is present as the beachfront ignites...

...She is walking her Father home...

"A Quiet Storm's Light"

Like a distant humming in a haze of smoky cloud,
Like a fire one can't see through the banks of foggy shroud,
Lest its flaming fingers claw,
It, a thunderless storm implodes,
And grows new branches of jaded, jagged chandeliers,
Flashing through the mountain ranges of humidity,
If it is silent in its own strength,
If in its dance of quiet light,
It remain,
Will the storm engulf this traveler,
With its sorrow and its sadness and its...

...Pain.

"Ultraviolet Life"

There is a dimension just beyond our human sight,
Like the resonating band of ultraviolet light,
It vibrates in its color,
Just like the reds and greens,
And the blues and the purples the human eye can see,
Yet just beyond that arch of visible light,
In the electromagnetic spectrum,
Lives this ethereal life;

She is sparkling like diamonds,
Sitting in this boat on Mother's Sea,
A million stars that crowd the night,
A million times more loving,
Than the sun for us its light;

She is radiating like a kaleidoscope of sunrises,
Pushed through the crowded tunnel of life,
She is sitting in this boat with her mother,
Just beyond her mother's sight,

"Keep rowing, Momma," she whispers,
"Until this boat takes flight..."

...Lavender silhouettes flash in tongues of flame,
As the salty waters splash against her windswept frame,
Calling her forward,
She rows...

"Listening to the Moon"

It speaks in ancient tongues,
Fires, its fragrance, spark the haunts of sky,
Where the blackness opens to a resonance sprung,
When the golden sphere breached the horizon line,
Blossoming scent of love and light,
That control the motions of the dancing tides,
And silver waves cascade over shadows,
As the ocean became one with the night;

She sang the praise of rugged, holy Saints,
And raised her eyes on high,
She gave her breath of light to light the way,
For those of heart and soul and mind,
She spoke with grace to grace those to save,
Those travelers on the waves of space and time,
And blessed us with an angel's kiss,
And Heaven set we are with mystical eyes,
Gazing upward to the giant orb that bobs up and down,
On massive waves,
And gaze upon her stabilizing, glowing soul,
That resonates with life,
Carrying her mother through choppy nights.

"Turquoise Diamonds Speak"

When deep in the meditation feel,
The reverence we together reveal...

...A motherlode of turquoise diamonds in every pore,
Like trillions of sand stars on millions of shores,
Alight within my skin,
Refracting the true life...

...Budding from the gardens from within.

"The Silver Glittering"

Fire beads and silver bracelets woven with liquid strings,
And stars,
Adorn her wrists with delicate, sparkling metals,
That accentuate the heart;

She with long white robes that glisten with the bands of silvery
moon,
Drape the waves as they crest and break,
Bursting flack and foam that blasts against the skiff,
In explosive salty bloom...

...There is a world beneath the stern of this skiff,
And swim, baby turtles, toward floral ocean dreams,
Beyond the swirling of the turbulent surf,
To sargassum gardens where the ocean breathes,
They swim into your hands,
Cupped as cradles that comfort the sea,
They rest on your fingers and lull to sleep in your peace,
Like blankets of summer moonlight...

...The threads of silver glittering.

"And What of the Oceans of Time"

Time - it is liquid, it streams,
Like rivers imbedded in ocean,
That drift in flow and lift in dream to dream,
But what of this dimension,
To truly live - we must press at the veil,
Pressure the cloak at its seams,
Threading our lives like stitches of tapestry,
Standing hand in hand in both worlds -

Sunset blend with sunrise,
You, with butterflies in your eyes,
And overflowing with love for me,
Gently combing my spirit with your breath,
And walking through me,
Through these spaces where time cannot forget,
Through the open country of my wounded soul,
Where you plant for your Mommy,
Acres of ocean flowers of pure gold,
A moment of beauty to help reconcile the grief;

And lifted higher, I can see,
That time - it is awash like the sea,
With waves that can never tame,
Nor capture you and me.

"The Treasure"

Wrap our collective arms around him, Mommy,
Invigorate his light,
He is joyous - he is strained,
He is porous rock - he has unique pain,
The shock that shook his life,
At twelve years old remains;

He is the treasure of the family, Mommy…

I visit him in his dreams,
On those nights he is caught in the slipstream,
When the nightmares come like contagions,
And he sobs within his sleep,
And hold him like he is a newborn,
Until he drifts back into peace;

For he is the treasure of the family, Mommy…

I walk with him through his waking days,
In the morning and through the dusk engaged,
With Daddy when the three of us play,
With the four of us when we sit and pray,
For he is my baby brother,
And I, though in a spiritual state,
Treasure him like no other,
For he is the treasure of the family, Mommy…

…Let us three be the ground beneath his feet.

"I Looked Tonight To The Sky For Answers"

Black waters above, the chasm of endless deep space,
Encrusted with tiny, distant, silver crystal flakes,
Like little opal lights that force themselves to flicker,
While drowned in ash and shale and inky, endless lakes;

Stringed necklaces of jeweled stellar flame,
Hung in patterns and constellation frames,
Emanate in hopeful, eternal bouquets,
Like diamonds clustered in icy chains;

Flowers for the centuries,
Flowers in the angel's hands,
Flowers she disperses to the winds,
As many the beach has grains of sand...

...Their soft, purple petals float back and forth,
Between these two worlds...

...And come to rest within my eyes.

"Purple Fields, Stars of Gold"

They are celestial flowers blooming in the sky,
Like Morning Glory on strings of nebula vine,
Sparkling,
Golden gems flash in dark purple fields,
Like fire in indigo eyes,
Fueled by the winds of the universe,
That swirl a galaxy into a soul,
That soul on the journey to the center of the spirit,
Gazing up at a nightly sky,
Purple fields, stars of gold…

…Were they a mere reflection,
Of the beautiful Exuma beach,
This is the image I convey to Daddy,
When he is quiet enough to see.

"Galaxies of Ocean Fire"

To the eye,
They were water droplets upon purple iris,
Tiny, delicate spheres,
Shiny, crystal tears,
Drenched in quiet, summer seaside garden;

Yet each its own flare,
Celestial spheres,
Globes of spirit water set afire by these souls,
Nestled together on floral, purple petals,
A galaxy of stars upon this sea flower glows,
As she gazes into the open waters,
And petals floating, drift by her slowly as she rows...

"After the Sunset, The Bloom It Keeps"

Smears of emotion, or torment, laced in scarlet bloom,
Shade into a deep golden hue,
There are dark blues,
And minty greens,
There are purples plumed,
And reconciliation to pursue,
And orange rifled streams,
In the sunset glowing,
The Master - He wakes again;

Evening, collapse unto the weight of a grieving sky,
Boiling with clouds that rise centuries high...

...Only there momentarily and seem to disappear,
From the limitations of the human eye,
After the sun sets the bloom, it speaks,
After the soul sets, the bloom, it keeps,
Its flame that goes on perpetually,
For you and I.

"Green Moon Clouds"

Ethereal veils of spectral velvet,
Crushed mint in effervescent brine,
They hang like regal emerald cloaks,
Across the black, electric sky,
Illuminated in the fury of the heat flash,
When the humid air and the lightning catch,
Spark in the wet heavy fields of thunder rash,
And a green mist lifts while the rain amassed,
In the storms above the ocean's womb,
Behold the true star…

She is like the Moon...

…The spirit guide that knows exactly who you are.

"Sea Salty Liquid Rainbows"

(i). "Steal Cut Water"

Rain slips from the gurgling oven,
Of overburdened cloud fields,
Shedding like skin flakes from the body,
As the layers lighten peel by peel;

Steal cut cubic tons of water,
That fill each tear that falls for my daughter,
With a weight that sinks the earthy crust,
And burns until the soul is crushed;

I stray, estranged from my own hour,
Swallowing swords in each gasp of breath,
Shocked with an accidental physical death,
In the dynamic prime of a youthful life,
Distanced from the chains of gladness,
Bonfires melt the sky with sadness,
As I curse the situation in its inherent cruelty,
And in its insatiable madness;

A tsunami in the void of kindness,
A sight line through a turbulent blindness,
A brine of swirling blue ocean and green tidal foam,
Shells break down in the churn,
They dust into sand upon which we may walk,
But upon which we must not construct a home,
For, other than this material,
There is a much Higher home;

(ii). "Harbor Approach"

...I scratch out a temple into the harbor,
And build a sanctuary, though it is harder,
To build upon the tides rather than lands,
To stretch out the skins across the platform,
And pray to your loving hands,
Half way between both worlds,
For that is where I can be with my girl;

(iii). Moon Diamonds

She was wearing moon diamonds in her golden hair,
And a white dress weaved with threads of stars encrusted,
As the musty smoke warmed and adjusted,
She emerged with the glow of a million suns,
And stood before me in her glory,
Smiling,
A stable of angels like sentries posted about her,
Holding her sacredly in divinity,
Watching over her and raising her human condition,
Into this much Higher home,
Built upon the rainbows of the sea,
Standing there in the distance on a distant beach...

...And I push forward through the breach.

"Waves of Light"

(i). Resting

Waves of light, blanket the badlands in solar wind,
and I in an emotionally derelict condition,
Try to harness the wind at my back,
A thunder chamber unhinged,
Trying my hardest for the light to convey me,
A hurricane breathes,
Lifting the sargassum and spinning the vegetation into
remorseful wreaths,
As the beach grows closer the waves conflict,
As the beach grows closer the veins restrict,
Until I nearly faint from the sadness,
And the excitement,
It blend;

The sun with beams of warmth caress the skin,
When the clouds pass to expose the holy orb,
Blazing across a blue sky,
Alight embraced in floral ocean dance,
I rest here momentarily to catch my breath,
A self-care moment of intervention,
Staring into the crosshairs of intersection,
Between opportunity and motherly intention;

(ii). Eternity of the Within

Lunar seas wash back and forth within my skin,
This human life giving way - is wearing thin,
It is temporary by immaculate design,
A gift to channel life as gifted by the Divine,
This shell, it is borrowed,
It is not mine;

The moment the road elevates into ether,
And the safeguards we've fabricated disrobe,
We are left with angel wings to emerge,
Never to navigate alone,
Our pores are each a crystal,
Through which a Galaxy illuminates,
The cells of our spirit skin,
When we physically die,
And spiritually transition,
From the eternity of the within;

(iii). Sea Steam

Drifting, I seem as if I was like steam,
On the sea drifting like sluggish seaweed,
Not a cloud in my mind,
To detract me,
The whimsical wave,
It attacks me,
And I don't care;

Blue shadows call amidst the shuffling in the headache,
It thumps to the beat of the vein of the heart,
As it tears itself apart,
In the drifting and the lifting of the sea steam,
I seem to conjure happy mirages,
And the years that should have been,
In the floating of the sea steam,
In the salt foaming webbing threads,
I roam;

Darwin's answer to an inhospitable exchange,
The fittest cog in the wheel of debate,
Makes the fittings for a cage,
And I rest amidst desisting this and cling to this refrain,
Never was a bone in my body built to lose this game.

"A Mother"

Dictating mayhem in the dawn of the crux of drowning
emotion,
For who dare a tiny wooden skiff in a thousand miles of ocean,
For who share the water stage with an agitated Poseidon,
Who clings to the gilded book of the gods for his caustic
devotion,
You sail directly across his face,
And down his throat,
And trigger his gag reflex,
As he throws up your boat,
The rudder scars the prove waves,
Leaving a white foamed jagged trace,
Of courage,
Of strength,
A mother,
A mother,
Need the sea god say more,
He lay his hands on the boiling sea,
And bridge a gap of calm,
For this mother to pass…

"This Eternity Torch"

This world,
Enslaved with joys that bathe dark troubles,
So hard at times to release,
Unleash,
Uncouple,
I walked into this paradox with a healthy skepticism,
Where the physical and spiritual hold a mystic rhythm,
I bathed in the rivers of fickle humility,
I gave and gave into the honor of talented thieves,
I sacrificed all selfish outlook in exchange for the greater good,
For it is in this greatness,
In which life's mystery could be understood,
Then the world with its random arbitrary sword,
Destroyed all that I cherished,
On this God forsaken road;

And these hands cup my armpits and lift my soul,
And she carries me across the minefield,
To a greater gold;

My child,
I hear you when the wind dies down,
I hear you when I lie fetal position still,
Exhausted on the wet planks in this hallowed ground,
As the water runs back and forth in guttural swill,
I die one thousand deaths a second,
And grief has yet to have its fill,
In each throbbing heart beat I scream,
And I bleed,
And I beckon,
For you,
My love;

Now you sit with me in your body of light,
(I can almost see you),
My lantern through the dark days,
Now blaze halos in the deepest night,
You speak in language only known to a mother and daughter,
Like breathing light that illuminates water,
Your mother searches for the edges to peel back the seam,
Your mother lurches forward in the afterglow,
Of a decadent dream,
For heartache's fingers have gripped my throat,
Though is hasn't seen the fury yet of a mother's grief explode;

You are fighting through the barriers of humanity's mesh,
Touching the light body that radiates under my human flesh,
You learn from the highest order of angels,
And convey God's wisdom through aerial angles,
That scorch the sky in lightning fingers,
Blistering in a violent flash and momentary linger,
That touch down within this heart...

...I will run through walls of earths for you,
Tear down the barricades of the universe,
Turn the oceans upside down,
And pound the mountains into flattened ground,
As I thrash about at emotional shadows in a violent accord,
Bleed these screams from the acrid pores,
Well blemished and torture scored,
Fall apart and see the water path,
That melts dimensions somehow,
Like staring into a crystal pool,
And seeing your lovely face looking back at me,
Refracting in the water,
Reflecting an inherent promise,
Fleeting, but leaving its trace,
Teaching me the eternity of now,
Teach me the eternity of now...

"In the Salty Fields"

In a brief respite,
Bequeath the frothy pulp of a maddening tear,
It is only one moment but it capitulate,
Into a chain that link the hour to day to month to year,
From sorrow to sadness to grief to total despair,
And decades before us still to sail,
Across the salty fields of a child's physical death;

Dream, drift and seethe,
On the oceans that one cannot imagine,
One cannot perceive,
For this one has been presented the station,
Of one who has been forsaken,
And weep in the caldron of the sea,
Keeper of longing and a broken hand that speaks,
In the salty fields the rash awakens,
And boils you down into a quiet dereliction,
Exhausted by experience and barely afloat,
And skinned raw red by the friction,
And grief that has you by the throat,
Stalked by bruising sentiment,
Flaunts your dismal weakened condition,
And taunts you in its deliberate goad,
To subjugate you in insufferable submission,
And toss you back into the tidal folds,
Until the salty fields,
Have claimed you as their own;

Dreaming Exuma,
The Infinite beach,
Dreaming of you on the shores of Exuma,
In the labyrinth of complexity,
Yet still within reach;

And how within the framework of human capacity,
Could a parent endure,
The torment, an enemy that bed in the skin,
Like ticks, their heads burrow nestled within,
Seeding disease in the mercurial host,
That flails about as the fever grows,
A new threat to a broken heart,
Suddenly a war cry erupts from the heavens…

…Onward,
We march…

"Body of Light"

If the stardust blankets the beaches,
If the stars are oceans of liquid light,
If the suns of the universe,
Were to form one embodiment of life,
It would be the love that flows through you,
A billion universes bright,
An angel of the highest order,
In her beautiful body of light.

"In Which The Higher Life Is Kept"

If the sun and this woman and this tempest strain,
Converge this heat, this steam, the thief that dance amongst the droplets,
Of the thieving rain,
Even the flora of the earth, it weeps for you,
And awash, the conscience gurgles,
Choking on the purpose and the total loss of meaning while it sleeps;

When even the sorrow, it struggles to make sense of this;

For the rest of my life whether awake or despondent deep,
I scream into the void in the hollow cords of grief,
Reaching for my daughter with empty hands,
In a pinnacle moment of horrific disbelief,
That rage from this nightmare that began in the street...

...The miracle is your presence, sweet Kayleigh,
For the sun - it never sets,
You are glory in this powerful transition,
In which your higher life is kept,
For while I know you now in two worlds,
I weep now as I have never wept,
For your innocent physical absence,
Has left me physically bereft,
For I am your mother,
In love with you, my child,
Let us stop here for a moment...

...And rest.

"A Welcome To Mother's Courage"

She lies quietly in the grips of intention,
Her gentle breaths are moistened prayers,
That lower the seas of tumultuous grief,
And as sure as the oceans seethe,
She will be undeterred,
Charting this course with belief;

Another day is set upon her;

Come, oh mountainous waters,
Typhoons and tsunamis and tidal waves,
Exploding against her frame,
Using her body like the bow of the boat,
Almost drowning her,
She who is afraid of drowning,
And parting in the explosions along her body,
As the waters peel the paint away,
She is still standing,
Standing, rooted to this skiff...

...For on the other side of this journey,
Her daughter calls her like a lighthouse,
Sparks in the deepest fog...

...And a path, it opens, stunting the storms,
Rolling water, bronzed with jaded stone flashing,
That lifts from the ocean's bottom,
As it offers its glistening bones,
To line the road,
With the gift of luminescence,
To light up each mile that leads her...

...To her daughter,
Though first she must in this ocean continue to go,
Deeply into its unpredictable currents,
That surround this Mother's soul...

...And in the next breath her daughter's face,
A smile, with prideful grace,
Welcomes her Mother's courage,
And each step forward that she takes.

"Jacob's Ladder's Broken Rung"

For all eyes with a heart look skyward;

The ladder is the reunion,
The bridge is the union,
The channel is communion,
The latter is the call;

For the ladder is the wooing,
For everything worth doing,
The holy angels are pursuing,
You,
To make sure that you don't fall;

For the ladder is reunion,
A bridge inside you brewing,
Longing to dare to dream,
Oh Lord,
To live within your eyes.

ASTRAL EXUMA EXTRAVIO

"A Theatre Of Dream Mirrors"

Finding oneself in a maze of stages,
With the footlights and the fog machines,
Billowing cloud fields and rainbow shards of tabby dust,
To blur the edges of these interlocking cages,
A year becomes another year,
Roped together in chains of metal tears,
While the spotlights draw in the audience,
The spectacle to observe in the center,
Fumbling blocking and miscuing lines,
The actor pervades in the shadows,
Where the mirrors mimic the fabrication...

...The fabrication of time.

"In The Nether Depths Of The Bottom Of The Mind's Fleeting Ocean"

Many are the mystical moments mayhem has moored,
Footed in the bedrock of the haunted human ecology,
Like oil slicks that cling to a virgin shore,
Like thousands of triggers bewitch psychology,
Lost in a million rooms without any floors,
We float among the faithless ghosts that fester in these soars,
And blanket the truth with any logical explanation,
Drowning all while treading water,
Then grasping sinking boulders as if they were salvation...

...They drag us to the bottom of this sea.

"Overtake This Mortal Shell"

Being pressed to the edges of my humanity,
My flesh is being turned into gold;

Compressed,
Although courage is pushing my light out from the inside,
Diamond sparkles of tiny light on my skin,
Pool in my pores;

What is beginning to shine on the outside,
Is that which resides within;

I am transforming, though years it may take to actualize,
As my body of light overtakes this mortal shell.

"We Are One"

For what is the pendulum and its staggering cost,
When heartache blurs the atmosphere,
And all hope is lost,
This contagion of agnosticism,
It flood the eyes with disassociation,
It creeps in through the grief,
And breeds fear that feeds spiritual rationalization,
Serving to weaken the connection,
A dereliction of actual reflection,
For with faith all hope is won,
I step back into your light,
And I find once again…

…That we are one,
We are one,
We are one.

"The Enchanting Wilds"

And I watch your loving intention,
And I love your loving smile,
And I meet you in the ascension,
Where you commune with your child,
And I light up your skin,
Like the sun drapes the beach for miles,
And I walk the within,
And hold you through your trials,
For I am, with loving intention,
The mirror image of your smile,
Your daughter, Mommy, I hear you,
I meet you in meditation...

...In the enchantment of the wilds.

"Ceili Cay, Exuma Infinite"

And into the shallows and through the noise of beachfront
waves,
Colors flashing in the intersession as the physical world,
And the spiritual world are, into each other, conveyed,
The dimensions melt into one flame,
As she slides the beaten skiff upon the white sand with a sudden
stop,
As the end of the rainbow opens to the soul its gaping mouth;

This island with its hidden bays,
And golden coves of light,
A beachfront with its pure white sand,
That illuminates the night,
Waters flow in turquoise sparkle,
That dance in the radiant sunbeams,
She stands there waving with excitement,
With a brilliant smile pressed to her face,
Leading her mother through, what seem like dreams,
But in reality prove to be,
Heaven's special place...

...For this special family.

"This Angel and the Ocean"

And I, who have been floating,
So many years - or many more,
And my knees now graze lightly,
Upon the bottom of a sandy shore,
My ears still floating in the currents,
Still floating towards that door,
The tidal shallows father me,
They gather me in glittering gold,
And push me gently like driftwood,
Upon this beach and its gentle floor,
That stretches out abundantly,
In radiance and light,
She took me by the hand,
To set my feet just right,
And walked me from the water's edge,
That glistened, warm and bright,
And kissed my soul as I stood upon,
The island of new life.

"We Are Rivers of Living Water II"

Stumbling out from under the smoldering vestibule,
Baptized like few, who have been thus challenged, defy,
She emerges as the battle dust settles,
As the death smoke subsides,
A warrior woman with a wound a moon mile wide,
It weeps like the Word of God from the hole in her side,
'I am here, Honey!' she cried -

"Then the angel showed me the river of the water of life,"
As bright as dancing crystals consuming light,
Flowing from the throne of God,
Blazing like a smoldering shooting star in flight,
Exploding into a bouquet of fire flowers that ignite your
moonlit eyes,
While a bashful earth, its poles upended,
Embarrassed with its floral disguise,
Bows reverently to this one,
As she pushes the equator aside,
"I knew you would come!"
She cried,
And confidently takes center stage,
And radiates as she reaches for her crippled hand,
And with the kiss of life, raises this woman,
Her mother, this warrior, this warrior who was,
As fierce in dedication as eternal love,
For her daughter...

...And together,
Out of their sparkling souls...

...Flow rivers of living water...

"Down Into the Seaside Soul"

In the effervescent chandeliers,
Where the diamond sands weave wind into these beaches,
There exists amongst the soft crests and dunes,
Where the reflective torches of the sparkling sun reaches,
Down into the seaside soul,
A voice of the sea,
A spirit of the sea...

...That leaves us overjoyed...

...And speechless.

"For At The Sea The Vibration is Higher"

In near silence the voice of the sea,
Speaks to the soul - and so clearly,
Tales of its mysteries,
Are given to those who believe,
And I believe in you -

...And liquid light pulses,
Through these minty sky fields,
These frontiers of golden country,
Where the spirit reveals,
Its truth -

...I was there awaiting, anticipating,
Your presence - your lovely entrance,
I sensed a shift in the doorway,
Lilac flavored and lavender scented,
Reminded me of the gardens of your youth,
And running down the path in flip flops,
And falling and chipping a tooth,
And clinging to me in my lap,
With my arms wrapped around you,
In love's authentic pursuit -

...And there I was,
Always with embrace,
Wiping the tears from your face,
And tiny blonde locks from your eyes,
My Love...

...Now as this cage looms to age me early,
With the tragedy that bucks and chokes and disturbs me,
And challenges me to rise and rise again,
I know an intuitive trick in the balance,
And a vow that I will always defend;

You are always present,
It is I - when in grief,
That blocks me from your whispers,
And the words that you speak,
That leaves me feeling helpless,
Though you are picking up my feet,
I know this,
I see this,
I feel this,
And together,
The vibration is higher,
When we are walking at the sea.

"Soul By Soul"

As if the tide has never shifted,
As if the time has known no toll,
We sit together staring at the sea,
A mother,
A daughter...

...Soul by soul.

"The Wind"

Its pulse - wax and wane,
Finds open window frame,
And breathes its prayer unto me;

Two women with long golden blonde hair,
That dances on the steady breeze,
On a sacred melody,
I listen - and then I see...

...Washing the weight from my feet,
Washing away today's grief,
Washing me into its sea,
Where the waters of wind, and time, overtake me...

...like a glistening prized shell on the beach,
It took many years to perfect you.

"Like a Hollow Bone"

Wind, a channel, walker, gentle steps taken,
Wind walker with soul ignited,
With spirit fully awakened,
Enter the doorway, the vessel,
Through the holy crown,
Like a hollow bone,
Spread your light within, and down...

...And fully throughout.

"Lavender Shores"

Once touched by angel feet the sand ignites,
Each footprint a blossom of granular light,
Sparking vibrantly and casting halos,
Purple radiance and pearly white;

You can see it from quite a distance,
Especially as haze on the summer sea night,
When the entire world is a blackness,
Except for this purple beacon burning bright;

And so with the dancing of the same two feet,
Across this beach a million times,
The Lavender Shores are a place of raw beauty,
That radiate as brilliantly…

…As the sun in the sky…

…Shines.

"Unbreakable"

Grind shell to sand,
And ancient dark green forest bands,
Emerge across the beach,
Years of flush tides,
Scrape off the eyes,
Like color is touched by bleach,
We walk, untethered, on this sea...

...Tumbling, small stones come to rest,
While ghost crabs tunnel for their nests,
The quiet overcomes you...

...And the heat...

...Trickling waves crash,
They rise and collapse,
And breathe upon the beach,
Leaving tangling seaweed,
And floral debris,
We search for treasures underneath...

...Late afternoon, silence, peace...

...Impressing our prints in the sand,
Smile in gentle laughter,
And miles to walk hand in hand...

...the promise we know.

"Along This Stretch Of Beach"

Velvet and frail,
With foamy white tails,
These waves break and breathe,
And the beach catches them,
And captures their gems,
Unfolding from their purple sheathes;

She unveils a host of brilliant truths,
Known little to mankind;

As the waters recede,
The sands shift and bleed,
And sing,
And blues and the turquoise emerge,
Leaving opal shells along this beach...

...I stand upon foundations of undefeated hope,
Foundations of burning jade and stone,
Foundations of all you give me,
That fills the chambers of my soul -

The brutality of the wounding, unconscionable,
The challenge before me untenable,
The minefield under feet is impossible to avoid,
The heartache that blooms is so plentiful,
It leaves miles of burning flowers to pull,
But even through the heartache,
I know that I will come to know,
Along this stretch of Exuma Infinite,
Walking with my daughter,
It will unfold...

...All of the hidden secrets of the soul.

"Meditation Beach"

Dark liquid lavender,
Oils of glossy painted light,
Alive across the night,
Where the ranges of stars,
Glitter like deep golden glassy shards,
Of the universe,
Laced in moonlight,
Yet it is midday,
Under the sun's brilliant blades,
Kissing the turquoise sea,
That foams lush and white,
And sinks into the impressions of our feet,
Upon this stretch of beach...

...There in the center,
This is no ordinary scene,
This is no figment of imagination nor a fragment of a dream,
It is you,
Standing and smiling on me,
Your long, golden hair blowing in the breeze,
You have shown me,
This place that knows me,
This place where our souls blend together into being.

"Water Bouquet"

Water bouquet,
Flowery spray,
The splash of sun drenched diamonds,
Ablaze;

Refractions of life,
Ribbons of light,
That live within the current,
And dance within the waves...

...A shimmering prism of colors catch,
Flickering with silver flecks as the waves collapse...

...And roll quietly under your feet.

"Blending Souls"

Blend aura's ethereal flesh,
And spiritual mesh,
Our streams of liquid light,
Weave together thread by thread;

Converge pink and white,
And become golden bright,
More together we are,
Than separate we are less...

...Divinity breathe us - we are home,
We in the blending of souls.

"Where the Turquoise Waters Rise"

The aqua, its lightning, rakes the salt from the shoal,
Oh dear Mother Nature, is your bounty not full,
Dream of a landscape not fit for human eyes,
Land on a dreamscape where the electric ocean...

...Flows...

...And the sandbars collide,
A tongue of eternity,
Stretches out from island's side,
We walk crystal white sands,
Where the turquoise waters rise;

The hum in the ocean, alive, green and icy blue,
It radiates like fire light escapes from the moon,
The artist, she chances a white golden hue,
And brushes the face of my canvas...

...Until the wounded eyes are renewed...

...With the love of a mother this child has assumed,
Painting with oils the shades of Exuma,
In mutual meditation pursued,
A spectrum I cannot see with my eyes,
An ethereal eternity that binds our lives,
Please be patient, for there are times...

...I cannot have my ear to the door of Heaven twenty four/seven,
I cannot twenty four hours a day be pressed to the gates of
Heaven...

...But I try,
I try,
I try...

"Starfish"

Autumn colors swirl in spring scented mist,
No season holds you bare,
Brown and teal mountains of cloud erode,
Converge in pinks and mint pastels,
Leathery blue sea burns in the distance,
As the golden sun singes the edge of horizon,
Setting it on fire and warming the air that streams toward us;

The waves are calm-less,
The waves roll on untethered,
The waves they rise and lower,
To the hand of Mother Weather,
I bank from moment to moment,
To sun, to gray,
To dark of night,
To enchanting midday,
Hallowed Moon, you sleep at noon,
Sleepy though awaken,
A starfish in a tidal pool laughs,
As the sun tickles its leggy frame,
Obscured by clouds a moment later,
Yet still it persists,
Just twenty feet from where we sit,
In just several feet of turquoise water,
Guiding my wayward and weary eyes,
While sitting with my daughter,
Hallowed Moon blink like a beacon,
A starfish in the sky.

"Leaning Into The Next Wave Together..."

Collapse of curled wave,
Explode with a spray,
Just you and me -

As we brace in towards,
The sea's tidal door,
Digging in our feet...

...We lean...

...And the waters recede under knees,
To gather again in the deep,
To gather again to sweep us away,
Yet it never can sweep us away -

And comes the next wave,
To crash in the wake,
Of the last water dream -

Our souls as our tether,
We lean in together,
And tame the wild sea...

...You and me.

"She Paints The Wild Clouds"

And, indelible, we pry,
Through the halls of waking spirit eye,
In hopes of glance that preys on the darkness,
For we need the breath of light,
For it teaches us, in spite,
Of the moments in this life we find to be heartless -

She rises, and rises - smiling on the halo of the sun,
She paints wild rainbows into the ribcage of clouds,
As the clouds, in their thunder tendencies, run,
Explode with echoes off into the horizon -

And, incredibly, we try,
Through the halls of drying eyes,
To emerge from the surge of grief and its darkness,
For with this, the bread of life,
We may see, though not with sight,
But with knowledge that we do not die,
And the strength to impart this -

She is here - call us to this higher ground,
To where the angels gather round,
Where only love and light and found,
Where she paints the wild clouds for her family...

"Beach Renewal"

Then I turn back toward the first truth of your physical death…

…With the day moon full and blued and the mood sullen and
subdued,
We walk along the ocean's gardens where the broken shells are
strewn,
And breathe salty air and embrace this tidal atmosphere,
You were waking,
You were standing there awake,
With the roaring waters curling at the break,
Bending in the wind,
That pressed the shore into your skin,
The scene quite revealing,
As shooting stars raced across the ceiling,
And crackled out of sight;

Indigo shadows,
Tucked into darker blue shallows,
Like hidden pools of soul scars that flurry in misty groans,
Wishing to remain uncharted, undiscovered and alone,
Danger - it lurks only in the corners of imagination's teeth,
But not on this desolate tropical track of beach,
With a bobbing buoy of dim light that glittered in the distance,
Providing the only signs of prying eyes -

We walk upon the sand and search for renewal,
And find that this life, though somewhat confusing and
seemingly cruel,
Gives enough for us to hold,
Gives us just enough to fill our souls…

…For the second truth, I am told,
Proves that you are here…

"Walking on Stars"

She points to a sector I haven't seen before,
And explained its significance;

Lakes of stars pool in the corners of the canthus,
And shoot across the uncharted oceans of our eyes,
Enchanted and ethereal,
A bridge of tears across the skies,
We find each other in our playgrounds of galaxies,
And embrace as deeply as the universe is wide,
We are, together, walking on stars,
The bond of which cannot one divide.

"On A Nightly Summer Beach"

Day and night merge and flash together;

Night softly clouds – towers of gray,
A beach blackness, webbed and blush,
Humid summer heated sky,
So wet the air to the touch,
Wind low, and it…

…Hush…

…Flashes in their smoky bellies,
A rage of white fire in jagged flight,
Lightning catches the distant sea within me,
By surprise,
Alight;

The stars sparkle across nebulous trails,
As we scan the Milky Way,
And its glittering tail,
Listen, the waves tumble on the beach,
As on the stars,
As night softly clouds roll passed our feet…

…On this nightly summer beach.

"Walk Upon the Wind That Walked Within My Soul"

I can feel the wind actually change in my soul,
That is how I know –

As it breathes across my skin I sense the energy grow,
That is how I know –

Because your love is immortal and eternal,
That is how I know -

For another - just a shift in the breeze,
A random act in the natural world,
For me and you, however, my girl,
There are times when the wind changes,
And that is how I know,
My daughter is walking,
And sailing the uncharted oceans of my soul.

"No Empty Space"

When I slow down the breath I better engage with your life,
For you are here,
Always here beside me,
There is no empty space,
Just a blending zone in this sacred place,
When you walk in the sun you cast a shadow of light.

"A Wilderness of Diamond Mirrors"

Saturn turns thunderous and the spectacle erupts;

Leaning into the fury of a jeweled downpour,
Stagger through this blizzard of jagged diamonds,
Harvested and hurled by the threatening storm,
Elevating the senses,
And thrown into the tempest of a grievous maelstrom;

A cross that few have been asked to carry,
I carry,
Its weight so burdensome,
Reshaping skin,
Deep in skin buried,
Sink further within,
It is imbedded squarely in my backbone;

I scream out into this curious basket of fright,
Peeling the ink from the shadows,
Just enough to see your face,
Emerge from these devastating rains...

...For you are the light in the lantern,
A heavenly rumination,
You are the muscle in the horse,
The catalyst of illumination,
You are the shelter from this storm,
A caregiver to a broken patient,
You are the hope that the bandages wrap,
In the wound that coagulation hastened;

I stagger and forward progress stalls,
I fall to my knees and crawl and crawl,
I lift to my feet to answer this fall,
And continue foreword,
To follow your call...

...Through the wilderness of diamond mirrors,
Lead me to your grace,
I open my eyes in the bowels of a deep breath,
And once again,
See your lovely face.

"Footprints on the Beaches of Jupiter"

Tiny footprints etch the sands of Jupiter,
Hidden beneath the swath of scarlet hurricanes,
A tea party in a grotto by a diamond river beach of light,
Watching the sunset glisten off of Ganymede's face;

On closer inspection,
The prints are from many ages,
And many different lives,
Yet the shapes, like fingerprints, tell the tail,
These are made by the same souls,
Four unique spirits traveling together,
From the edge of the universe to the lift of the beyond,
Where illumination always holds their sway,
And opens doors to a million chambers...

...That channel the Milky Way.

"Comfort"

Throw to me your waves of light,
Like blankets of threading glowing bright,
To wrap around my soul and flesh,
And merge into my human mesh.

"Pelican-Like"

(i). The Sacrificial Self

Shall you pierce your breast with your beak,
Releasing the blood of life,
Feeding the children whose hunger,
Echoes through the night;

Nourishing the babies,
Feeding them one's body,
They drink the purity of light,
And selflessly we learn this trait,
If we are Pelican-like;

With nobility and elegance,
Quite aware and intentional with this sacrifice,
Always reliable, sensible,
Always quite focused in spite,
Of a world that slips from its own sanity,
I return to being Pelican-like;

(ii). Resurrecting

Gracefully swooping through the space of the audience of the
Moon,
She smiles on His flight,
She knows His every mannerism,
His meaning, His sacrifice,
And loves Him with perfect reverence,
All glory she hands to Him;

(iii). Winged Bird of Air and Water

There is an emotional sea that fluctuates,
Its sustenance abounding,
Winged bird high about the air,
Soaring silently towards the waves,
Banking as You disappear,
Fill Your bill with sea salty spray and waters,
Reconnect and reclaim your grounding,
The heart with the mind,
And you shall find,
The balance;

(iv). Diving Deeply Into the Sea

Both air and water creatures,
Of thought and emotion and subliminal features,
These variables between heart and mind,
The sea above the sky and the sky below the ocean,
Diving deepest into waters for its sustenance,
A nose dive into the deepest waters of the soul,
For it is in the seeking,
And only in the seeking,
That we will find what we have already known,
And know already what we will find.

"Under The Safety of a SuperMoon"

In the breath of the wind,
Where the moon finds its twinkling eyes,
And the lights crescendo like halos,
Just beyond the sound of my cries,
Though the enchanting glow it warms me so,
I have been struck by one million pains,
That rip my earth apart like one thousand hurricanes,
Tied together in my soul;

Yet the night is my sanctuary with you,
In your miraculous hold,
And I, through my trembling and sullen groans,
Weep and screech and scream into the void,
Underneath a SuperMoon,
Where I search for your touch,
That I trust will bloom,
Not always when I summon it,
But soon;

I still myself in meditative glances,
And then in the wind chimes,
In the fresh scented branches,
I hear the compassion of your voice,
Living our lives together as only we can,
Facing the worst or the worst of circumstances,
Kissing my ear and filling my soul,
With intention,
With devotion,
With a blending of our spirits,
Two streams of God's liquid gold,
Cast in the mold of the SuperMoon,
Where in each other...

...We are home.

"Lavender Shores"

Once touched by angel feet the sand ignites,
Each footprint a blossom of granular light,
Sparking vibrantly and casting halos,
Purple radiance and pearly white;

You can see it from quite a distance,
Especially as haze on the summer sea night,
When the entire world is a blackness,
Except for this purple beacon burning bright;

And so with the dancing on the same two feet,
Across this beach a million times,
The Lavender Shores are a place of raw beauty,
That radiate as brilliantly as the sun in the sky shines.

"In the Glory of the Afterglow"

As crystal rash spread in water,
With a heated, humid, afterglow,
Illuminating ice green turquoise,
And clouds that spark of minty indigo,
It bled over coral, rocks and jagged shoals,
And spread in the crevasses,
Refracting as it grows,
Beaming in the sunlight,
Where shiny diamonds laugh and dance,
In the glory of the afterglow,
Spreads a crystal water rash.

"On This Angelic Road..."

In this human dimension the optics are limited,
Though not an optical illusion,
In the sky caps of higher dimension,
In the kaleidoscope of ascension,
Where the colors crash and blend and glow,
And this life can mimic an intrusion,
In the expanse of this astral tunnel,
Along the edges of angelic road,
I see the vestige of my lives flash and flow,
Like a living spark that illuminates a window,
And in this halo of allusion...

...I see my higher life.

"Where You Find Peace"

Breathe the healing light of the world,
And be the healing light so that others may breathe;

Retreat not into the saturation,
Where the ego displays its shiny objects,
Do not wallow in the folly and the fabric it deceives;

Rather, it is for you to harness your passionate spirit,
And let the selfish habits, like captured water,
Drain from open fingers,
To return to the flowing oceans of the mind,
Where, alas, against your eager wishes, you find peace.

"A Bridge of Light"

A flood of brilliant liquid lightning,
It radiates this intended air,
Illuminated brightly,
In this vibrant atmosphere;

Eternal cord - it merges souls,
Strengthens in the love we share,
No space - nor distance can be tolled,
And golden streaks wrapped in your hair,
Like galaxies and celestial flairs,
They resonate in all we dare,
A mommy and her daughter here…

…Laughing on the world.

"Soul Embrace"

And as our hands touch,
And our fingers intertwine...

...Explodes a flash of brilliant rippling white light,
As our souls embrace,
As our souls ignite,
Together making a blinding sunny day,
Out of the fomenting ink of night,
Where nothing is impossible,
As we, arm in arm...

...Embrace the current steps upon the journey of this life,
This life,
This current life.

"My Love Song To You"

My love song to you is simply my life,
The days ahead,
The flows and ebbs,
The gardens tending,
Wounds amending,
Through the triumph and the strife,
My love song to you is how I treat my life -

A thieving grievance bites to shun me,
A forbearance scores my earth,
A poison fills the lowlands and leads to my sea,
I will tend to that also because,
My Love, you see,
My love song is the condition of my life,
To which I have bequeathed,
My gift of me to you -

I will not leave this human skin,
Leaving a debris field of my country within,
Leaving a wretched wreck on the pristine shores of your soul,
No, no - I will not dishonor you,
I will offer you light, and love to behold,
By churning my wounded spirit into luminous gold,
By each step that I take here,
With intention - with this goal,
I write my love song to you,
As we walk the remainder of my difficult road.

"Boat of Light"

And I traveled in a boat of light,
Planked by the beams of sunrise and sunset,
Nailed through each board with the experiences of life,
And designed to face the oceans I haven't tested yet;

It was in that instant of flight,
When I stepped into the ribcage of that holy night,
Blessed with those on each side of the veil,
I took my first breath and then I set sail;

Traveling in a boat of pure light,
Finding the waters will give me no fight,
Except for the fight in my heart and my mind,
I arrived within sunrise and the sunset alive,
In the glory of the blink of a well lived human life.

"Little Baby Rainbows"

With a delicate smile, Kayleigh reached behind her to what seemed a few feet, but was in reality twenty miles, and plucked a tiny rainbow from the sky. It shimmered in her hands, bending up from one palm and arching over smoothly down into the other. It was like a slinky in its dexterity and like a child's slime in texture, but pure, otherworldly light. Quite impossible for a human mind to understand, but just perfect.

"Mommy, I showed Daddy when he was here. He just stared into my hands with a hilarious grin on his face. You know Daddy and that face!"

She lowered her left hand and raised her right, back and forth, manipulating its length and shape and brightness. "Aren't they cute, Mommy? They bounce around or are sleepy in your palms, flexible, bendy little baby rainbows filled with radiant light. You just cradle them in your hand or set them free into the breeze or set them into the distant sky and they expand and melt and blossom and radiate and become ever more vibrant in their bands of color. Sometimes they melt into jellyfish lanterns. The space whales love them! They are amazing! I love it here in Exuma Infinite! I love when you can manage to make it here to Exuma Infinite in these dedicated meditations. And I love it here by your side on this physical plain in my body of light."

I love it here, Kayleigh, we all love it here. When we catch glimpses of Ceili Cay, the island you named after yourself. Your father has explained it to me. Shown me his vision you've given him in your writings together. But to see it with my own spirit eye, it is indescribable. Please show your brother as well. He

123

needs to see this. He's so smart, Kayleigh, like you. And he feels you constantly.

"I love my baby brother so much! I will make sure I show him. It'll have to be in a visitation, like a Jedi mind trick, you know? Since he doesn't meditate really. Not yet at least. I can catch him in his sleep. I promise, Mommy."

I know you will, Honey. I love you, Kayleigh. I am here. I have crossed this sea. I have withstood enormous waves. I have even built this skiff for the crossing. Nails of grief. With my flesh and blood. With my motherly ribcage. My womb. With faith and through feelings of being forlorn. Desolation. Despondency for miles. Brief encounters with light. Through it all. Nothing, Kakes, can keep me away from my babies. And you, now in spirit, nothing will keep me from trying. From making it to your side.

"And Mommy, nothing, not even my physical death and physical absence, nothing will ever keep me away or apart or distant from you. You are my mother. My mother. And I am so, so deeply in love with you. Love you, Mommy."